Bewa
Hypocrisy

A commentary of Sūrah Munāfiqūn which discusses the treacherous evil habits of the hypocrites which every believer should avoid at all cost.

By

Shaykh Mufti Saiful Islām

JKN Publications

First Published in July 2020

ISBN 978-1-909114-56-2

British Library Cataloguing in Publication Data
A catalogue record for this book is available from the British Library.

Publisher's Note:

Every care and attention has been put into the production of this book. If however, you find any errors they are our own, for which we seek Allāh's ﷻ forgiveness and reader's pardon.

Published by:

JKN Publications
118 Manningham Lane
Bradford
West Yorkshire
BD8 7JF
United Kingdom

t: +44 (0) 1274 308 456 | w: www.jkn.org.uk | e: info@jkn.org.uk

Book Title: Beware of Hypocrisy

Author: Shaykh Mufti Saiful Islām

Printed by Mega Printing in Turkey

بسم الله الرحمن الرحيم

"In the Name of Allāh, the Most Beneficent,
the Most Merciful"

Contents

Introduction

All praises are to Allāh ﷿, the Most Merciful the Most High. Glory be to Him who bestowed upon us His Dīn and the holy Qur'ān through which we have been given many valuable lessons. Peace and blessing upon our last and final Prophet Muhammad ﷺ through whom this religion has reached us in its true form. May Allāh ﷿ reward the Sahābah رضي الله عنهم and the Tābi'īn and all those after them who continue to spread the one true religion of Islām, Āmīn.

The holy Qur'ān is the only heavenly book which has maintained its true form without any change from human or Jinn, for this we should be very grateful. It has lessons within it to guide Muslims how we should live our lives day to day and how we can become the best versions of ourselves through religion and spirituality. If we were to follow the advice and instructions that Allāh ﷿ has given us in the Qur'ān, then our lives would be much eaiser to handle. The holy Qur'ān has many rights over us whether it be for us to read it constantly or to understand the resposibilties which are upon us and for us to fulfill them by seeking a means of learning the teachings of the Qur'ān.

Daily recital of the Qur'ān guarantees ease in our daily obstacles and creates a lifelong friendship that you can rely on in times of happiness and in difficulty. Allāh ﷿ sent the Qur'ān to us so that we take heed from it, but we have abandoned it and made it become an ornament in our homes. We open it for only one month in the year, then for the rest it returns to its status of decoration again.

I pray to Allāh that we create a bond with the holy Qur'ān which will remain till our last breath and that it becomes a means of salvation for us on the Day of Judgement.

May Allāh reward every person who helped write this book in this world and in the hereafter, May we all take lessons from what is within it and understand the beautiful teachings of Allāh through it. May Allāh grant Shaykh Mufti Saiful Islām goodness in this world and in the hereafter and accept him for all his efforts. Āmīn.

Apa Khansā Nawāz
Graduate of JKN 2019
Ramadhān 1441/May 2020

Life of the holy Prophet ﷺ in Madīnah

When the holy Prophet ﷺ came to Madīnah, the two main tribes that were present were the Khazraj and Aws. He found a safe haven amongst them as they promised to defend him. The holy Prophet ﷺ as he was the most honourable and noblest of all people; became the rightful leader of their people.

Prior to his coming, the people of Madīnah had been deliberating of turning Madīnah into a kingdom and crowning 'Abdullāh ibn Ubbay ibn Salūl their king, but this did not take place as the people of Madīnah began to embrace Islām, and then when the holy Prophet ﷺ came to Madīnah , the people immediately made him their leader. This caused a deep-rooted resentment and burning rage to grow within the heart of 'Abdullāh ibn Ubay, as he felt that the holy Prophet ﷺ had robbed him of his kingship. The vast majority of people had accepted Islām and declared the holy Prophet ﷺ their leader. He felt that he had no option but to comply in following the people in his acceptance of faith, despite his deeply felt hatred of the holy Prophet ﷺ which was ingrained in his heart; a far cry from true belief as he feigned his declaration of faith in front of the holy Prophet ﷺ and the believers.

The Munāfiqūn (hypocrites) were a group of people who did not have the courage to openly oppose the holy Prophet ﷺ feeling that it would be unfavourable in their favour if they wished to find a way of overpowering the Muslims. They felt that they had to wait for the right moment and opportunity to present itself before they made their move, and this is what we witness throughout the course of action they took.

Time and time again, when they felt that the opportunity was correct, they wasted no time in causing mischief and planting seeds of rebellion within the ranks of the Muslims. Outwardly, they professed faith and rallied around the believers in a facade of showing their support. They would join the daily salāh (prayer) and all the other acts of worship that the believers engaged in, in order to avert suspicion. In fact, their outward behaviour was so impressive that Allāh ﷻ revealed the following verse warning the holy Prophet ﷺ:

وَإِذَا رَأَيْتَهُمْ تُعْجِبُكَ أَجْسَامُهُمْ ۖ وَإِن يَقُولُوا تَسْمَعْ لِقَوْلِهِمْ ۖ

"When you look at them their physical appearance appeals to you and when they speak, you listen attentively to what they have to say." (63:4)

Allāh ﷻ then revealed verses alerting the believers in unveiling the truth about their presence and the hypocrisy they concealed within their hearts. Allāh ﷻ says:

إِنَّ الْمُنَافِقِينَ يُخَادِعُونَ اللَّهَ وَهُوَ خَادِعُهُمْ وَإِذَا قَامُوا إِلَى الصَّلَاةِ قَامُوا كُسَالَىٰ يُرَاءُونَ
النَّاسَ وَلَا يَذْكُرُونَ اللَّهَ إِلَّا قَلِيلًا ﴿١٤٢﴾ مُّذَبْذَبِينَ بَيْنَ ذَٰلِكَ لَا إِلَىٰ هَٰؤُلَاءِ وَلَا إِلَىٰ

هَٰٓؤُلَآءِ ۚ وَمَن يُضۡلِلِ ٱللَّهُ فَلَن تَجِدَ لَهُۥ سَبِيلٗا ﴿١٤٣﴾

"Indeed, the hypocrites (try to) deceive Allāh whereas He deceives them. When they stand up for salāh, they stand up lazily, to show people and they remember Allāh only a little. Swaying between (īmān and disbelief), they are neither towards these (the believers), nor towards those (the disbelievers). You shall never find a way for him whom Allāh has led astray." (4:142-143)

The hypocrites lacked the courage to endure dangerous or unpleasant things. The signs of hypocrisy became evident and physically distinctive in the battle of Uhud, 'Abdullāh ibn Ubay withdrew from the battlefield along with 300 of his men, leaving the Muslim army of 700 men to face an army of 3000 men of the opposing force. He made the excuse that the holy Prophet ﷺ had not considered his request and as a result, he left taking with him all his men. In the most critical times when the holy Prophet ﷺ required their support, they always found a way of deserting the holy Prophet ﷺ at his greatest time of need. Despite this, the holy Prophet ﷺalways overlooked their faults. Even during this stage, when some of the Companions ؓ approached 'Abdullāh ibn Ubay and said to go and ask the holy Prophet ﷺ to pray for his forgiveness, he refused to comply.

In the expedition against the tribe of Banū Nadhīr, 'Abdullāh ibn Ubay secretly sent messages to the Jews that they were with them and that they would fully support them. In reality the hypocrites hoped that the Jews would put an end to the Muslims and destroy them once and for all. This is mentioned in the following verse:

أَلَمْ تَرَ إِلَى الَّذِينَ نَافَقُوا يَقُولُونَ لِإِخْوَانِهِمُ الَّذِينَ كَفَرُوا مِنْ أَهْلِ الْكِتَابِ لَئِنْ أُخْرِجْتُمْ
لَنَخْرُجَنَّ مَعَكُمْ وَلَا نُطِيعُ فِيكُمْ أَحَدًا أَبَدًا وَإِنْ قُوتِلْتُمْ لَنَنْصُرَنَّكُمْ وَاللَّهُ يَشْهَدُ
إِنَّهُمْ لَكَاذِبُونَ ﴿١١﴾ لَئِنْ أُخْرِجُوا لَا يَخْرُجُونَ مَعَهُمْ وَلَئِنْ قُوتِلُوا لَا يَنْصُرُونَهُمْ
وَلَئِنْ نَصَرُوهُمْ لَيُوَلُّنَّ الْأَدْبَارَ ثُمَّ لَا يُنْصَرُونَ ﴿١٢﴾ لَأَنْتُمْ أَشَدُّ رَهْبَةً فِي صُدُورِهِمْ مِنَ
اللَّهِ ذَٰلِكَ بِأَنَّهُمْ قَوْمٌ لَا يَفْقَهُونَ ﴿١٣﴾

"Have you not seen the hypocrites who say to their disbelieving brothers of the People of the Book, 'If you are exiled, we shall definitely leave with you and we shall never obey the word of anyone concerning you. We shall also certainly assist you if you are fought.' Allāh testifies that they are certainly liars. If they are exiled, they will not leave with them and if they are engaged in battle, they will not assist them. Even if they must assist them, they will surely turn their backs after which they will not have any assistance. Without doubt the fear they have in their hearts for you is more than the fear they have for Allāh. This is because they are a nation that has no understanding." (59:11-13)

They thought they were deceiving Allāh ﷻ by acting as believers, but Allāh ﷻ was aware of their disloyalty and betrayal. Their identity was slowly becoming unravelled in front of the believers as their outward bursts of hatred and fury exhibited itself from time to time, when they could not contain their outrage.

This reached its peak on the return from the expedition of Banū Mustaliq. An argument had broken out between two people; one of them was from the Muhājirūn and the other belonged to the Ansār. The man from the tribe of the Muhājirūn called out for help from his fellow tribesmen and the Ansārī man did likewise; each person rallying their tribes around them in support. This began to escalate and had the holy Prophet ﷺ not intervened and diffused the situation, this would have resulted in a full-fledged battle. It was only after the holy Prophet ﷺ had rebuked them that the people realised their mistakes and immediately sought forgiveness and made amends.

This did not go unnoticed by 'Abdullāh ibn Ubay; providing him with the golden opportunity in convincing the people of Madīnah to expel the migrants of Makkah. He set upon his task in attempting to convince them. His deceitful plans were exposed when a young Sahābī boy had overhead him and immediately informed the holy Prophet ﷺ. 'Abdullāh ibn Ubay tried to cover his tracks by saying that this was only the word of a boy and how could the holy Prophet ﷺ could even think of taking his word over his. However, revelation descended, and the young sahābī boy's statement proved true. 'Abdullāh ibn Ubay's deceitful lies were exposed out into the open. Even after this the holy Prophet ﷺ took no decisive action against him and let things be.

Not long after, 'Abdullāh ibn Ubay passed away. His son insisted for the holy Prophet ﷺ to lead his Janāzah (funeral) prayer to which the holy Prophet ﷺ accepted. It was only after this incident that Allāh ﷻ

revealed a verse instructing the holy Prophet ﷺ not to pray the Janāzah prayer or stand over the graves of those who had died as a Munāfiq (hypocrite). The holy Prophet ﷺ tried his utmost in an attempt to win their hearts over into accepting Islām, but each time he made the effort, they further intensified their hostility. In the end, Allāh ﷻ revealed a verse instructing that they had transgressed beyond bounds, and this should become evident in the way the holy Prophet ﷺ dealt with them; i.e. in not leading their funeral prayer or displaying any form of sympathy towards them.

Up until this point the holy Prophet ﷺ had shown them nothing except compassion and mercy, to the extent that when the leader of the hypocrites died, in addition to praying his Janāzah prayer, he even allowed him to be buried in his own blessed garment at the request of ʻAbdullāh ibn Ubay's son.

This is where the line had to be drawn as Allāh ﷻ revealed a verse forbidding the holy Prophet ﷺ to lead their prayers or even stand at their graves. It was one thing to openly declare rejection of faith but then to disbelieve and then show belief was a serious level of deceit and deception which would carry a greater level of penalty. Allāh ﷻ says in the Qur'ān:

إِنَّ الْمُنَافِقِينَ فِي الدَّرْكِ الْأَسْفَلِ مِنَ النَّارِ ۚ وَلَن تَجِدَ لَهُمْ نَصِيرًا ۝

"Most assuredly, the hypocrites shall be in the lowest depth of the Fire and you will never find a helper for them." (4:145)

وَعَدَ اللّٰهُ الْمُنٰفِقِيْنَ وَالْمُنٰفِقٰتِ وَالْكُفَّارَ نَارَ جَهَنَّمَ خٰلِدِيْنَ فِيْهَا ؕ هِيَ حَسْبُهُمْ ۚ وَلَعَنَهُمُ اللّٰهُ
وَلَهُمْ عَذَابٌ مُّقِيْمٌ ۝

"Allāh promises the fire of Jahannam for the hypocrite men, the hypocrite women and the disbelievers. They shall live there forever. It is enough for them. Allāh has cursed them and they shall suffer an everlasting punishment." (9:68)

Allāh ﷻ describes the hypocrites in the Qur'ān by saying:

اَلْمُنٰفِقُوْنَ وَالْمُنٰفِقٰتُ بَعْضُهُمْ مِّنْۢ بَعْضٍ ۘ يَاْمُرُوْنَ بِالْمُنْكَرِ وَيَنْهَوْنَ عَنِ الْمَعْرُوْفِ
وَيَقْبِضُوْنَ اَيْدِيَهُمْ ؕ نَسُوا اللّٰهَ فَنَسِيَهُمْ ؕ اِنَّ الْمُنٰفِقِيْنَ هُمُ الْفٰسِقُوْنَ ۝

"The hypocrite men and women are from each other. They command evil, prevent good and withhold their hands. They forget Allāh, and He does not bother with them. Indeed, the hypocrites are the sinners." (9:67)

The hypocrites were referred to as being two-faced. Outwardly they feigned belief but inwardly they opposed the holy Prophet ﷺ.

Sayyidunā 'Ammār ؓ reported that the Messenger of Allāh ﷺ said:

مَنْ كَانَ لَهُ وَجْهَانِ فِي الدُّنْيَا كَانَ لَهُ يَوْمَ الْقِيَامَةِ لِسَانَانِ مِنْ نَارٍ

"Whoever carries two faces in the world, he will have two tongues of fire on the Day of Resurrection." (Abū Dāwūd)

Scholars have mentioned that there are two types of Nifāq (hypocrisy). The first type is اَلنِّفَاقُ الْاِعْتِقَادِيُّ (Nifāq-e-I'tiqādi) - hypocrisy in faith. Within this group there are six different types:

	Type of Hypocrisy	Definition:
1	تَكْذِيْبُ الرَّسُوْلِ Takdhībur Rasūl	To deny the holy Prophet ﷺ
2	تَكْذِيْبُ بَعْضِ مَا جَاءَ بِهِ الرَّسُوْلُ Takdhīb Ba'dī Mā Jā'a Bihir Rasūl	To deny some of the articles brought by the holy Prophet ﷺ.
3	بُغْضُ الرَّسُوْلِ Bughdur Rasūl	To have hatred for the Messenger of Allāh ﷺ.
4	بُغْضُ بَعْضِ مَا جَاءَ بِهِ الرَّسُوْلُ Bugdhu Ba'di Mā Jā'a 'Bihir Rasūl	To have hatred for some of the articles of faith brought by the holy Prophet ﷺ.
5	اَلْمَسَرَّةُ بِاِنْخِفَاضِ دِيْنِ الرَّسُوْلِ Al Masarrātu Bi-in Khifād Dīnīr Rasūl	Displaying happiness upon the matter of the Dīn of Allāh ﷻ being suppressed.
6	اَلْكَرَاهِيَّةُ لِاِنْتِصَارِ دِيْنِ الرَّسُوْلِ Al Karāhiyyath Li-Intisāri Dīnir Rasūl	To dislike that the Dīn of Allāh ﷻ is being victorious.

The second type of hypocrisy is اَلنِّفَاقُ الْعَمَلِيّ (Nifāq Amalī) – hypocrisy in action.

Sayyidunā Abū Hurairah ﷺ reported that the Messenger of Allāh ﷺ said:

آيَةُ الْمُنَافِقِ ثَلَاثٌ إِذَا حَدَّثَ كَذَبَ وَإِذَا وَعَدَ أَخْلَفَ وَإِذَا اؤْتُمِنَ خَانَ

"The signs of a hypocrite are three: when he speaks, he lies, when he gives a promise, he breaks it and when he is trusted he betrays." (Bukhārī)

Many a times, we are oblivious to the severity of lying. In our daily conversations, many statements which contain lies are uttered without feeling the slightest remorse or guilt at our action of being dishonest.

Once the holy Prophet ﷺ visited a house when he heard a mother calling her child to come towards her. The child remained inattentive, so the mother called out again, only this time saying to come towards her as she had something in her hand that she wanted to give to the child. The holy Prophet ﷺ upon hearing this approached the woman and asked if she really did have something which she was going to give to her child. When she replied she had, the holy Prophet ﷺ replied that had she not given something to her child then this would have been written as a lie against her.

At times, parents promise to give their children a reward should they carry out a particular action but when the child fulfils in carrying this out, the parents fail to keep their word. Not only will this be a lie written against them, but they have also failed in keeping their promise which is another act of transgression. These things we may regard as petty and insignificant but in the court of Allāh ﷻ they are serious beyond what we could possibly imagine.

Another characteristic that the holy Prophet ﷺ mentioned of a hypocrite was: *"When he argues, he uses foul language." (Muslim)*

Allāh ﷻ says:

وَمِنَ النَّاسِ مَن يَقُولُ آمَنَّا بِاللَّهِ وَبِالْيَوْمِ الْآخِرِ وَمَا هُم بِمُؤْمِنِينَ ﴿٨﴾ يُخَادِعُونَ اللَّهَ
وَالَّذِينَ آمَنُوا ۚ وَمَا يَخْدَعُونَ إِلَّا أَنفُسَهُمْ وَمَا يَشْعُرُونَ ﴿٩﴾ فِي قُلُوبِهِم مَّرَضٌ
فَزَادَهُمُ اللَّهُ مَرَضًا ۖ وَلَهُمْ عَذَابٌ أَلِيمٌ بِمَا كَانُوا يَكْذِبُونَ ﴿١٠﴾

"Amongst people there are those (the hypocrites) who say, 'We believe in Allāh and in the Final Day,' whereas they are not believers. They (attempt to) fool Allāh and the believers but they only fool themselves without realising it. A disease is in their hearts and Allāh increases their disease. They shall suffer a painful punishment on account of the lies they speak." (2: 8-10)

إِذَا جَاءَكَ الْمُنَافِقُونَ قَالُوا نَشْهَدُ إِنَّكَ لَرَسُولُ اللَّهِ ۗ وَاللَّهُ يَعْلَمُ إِنَّكَ لَرَسُولُهُ وَاللَّهُ يَشْهَدُ
إِنَّ الْمُنَافِقِينَ لَكَاذِبُونَ ﴿﴾

"When the Munāfiqūn come to you they say, 'We testify that you

are certainly Allāh's Messenger.' Allāh knows well that you are His Messenger and Allāh testifies that the Munāfiqūn are liars." (63:1)

The Munāfiqūn would try to hide their hypocrisy and in front of the holy Prophet ﷺ put on a deceptive act of being pious and obedient in obeying him. Deep down they resented the holy Prophet ﷺ and their hearts were full of hatred towards him. On the surface they would profess to be believers, but their faith did not penetrate their hearts.

There are different categories of people:

1. The disbelievers – they do not proclaim belief nor do they possess faith within their hearts.
2. The hypocrites – they proclaim faith with their tongues but in their hearts, they possess disbelief.
3. Ahle Kitāb – they are the People of the Book who knew in their hearts that the message was the truth, but they disbelieved.
4. True believers – they affirm the truth by their tongue which is also testified by their heart.

Regarding the People of the Book, Allāh سبحانه وتعالى says in the Qur'ān:

ٱلَّذِينَ ءَاتَيۡنَٰهُمُ ٱلۡكِتَٰبَ يَعۡرِفُونَهُۥ كَمَا يَعۡرِفُونَ أَبۡنَآءَهُمۡ ۞

"Those who have been given the Book (Jews and Christians) recognise him like they recognise their own (sons) children. (2:146)

Sayyidunā 'Umar رضي الله عنه added that these people were convinced beyond doubt that the holy Prophet ﷺ was indeed the final Messenger who was described in their Books, because regarding their own wives there could exist the possibility of infidelity and as a result the child may not be theirs, but regarding the holy Prophet ﷺ there was no shadow of doubt:

وَجَحَدُوا بِهَا وَاسْتَيْقَنَتْهَا أَنفُسُهُمْ ظُلْمًا وَعُلُوًّا ۚ فَانظُرْ كَيْفَ كَانَ عَاقِبَةُ الْمُفْسِدِينَ ۝

"They unjustly and arrogantly rejected them whereas their souls were convinced about them. So, see what the outcome was of those who caused corruption." (27:14)

اتَّخَذُوا أَيْمَانَهُمْ جُنَّةً فَصَدُّوا عَن سَبِيلِ اللَّهِ ۚ إِنَّهُمْ سَاءَ مَا كَانُوا يَعْمَلُونَ ۝

"They use their oaths as shields and prevent (others) from Allāh's path. Evil indeed is that which they do." (63:2)

The word Junnah refers to a shield and the Munāfiqūn would use the proclamation of faith to shield themselves from adversities and external enemies.

The word Junnah is made up of the Arabic letters Jīm and Nūn. Any Arabic word which is made up of these two letters has an element of concealment within its meaning. For example, Junnah is a shield used to conceal or hide oneself from the enemy. Other examples include:

1. Jinn – a creation of Allāh ﷻ which is hidden from our eyes.
2. Jannah – this refers to Paradise which is concealed from our

eyes.

3. Janīn – the foetus which is hidden in the mother's womb.
4. Junūn – madness which is concealed in a person's mind.

The holy Prophet ﷺ was from the tribe of Quraysh and the Jews had always been under the impression that the Prophet would be from their own lineage and so this was the reason why they rejected him. They could not fathom that someone who was not from their own tribe and creed could proclaim prophethood for himself. They felt their own tribe and community was far superior, so they felt that they could not accept a prophet of a descent and lineage which was foreign to theirs, and hence rejected him outright despite recognising him of possessing all the visible signs of prophet hood.

The Believer's Honour is Sacred

Those who accepted faith were honoured and accepted as part of the group of believers:

الَّذِينَ يَتَّبِعُونَ الرَّسُولَ النَّبِيَّ الْأُمِّيَّ الَّذِي يَجِدُونَهُ مَكْتُوبًا عِنْدَهُمْ فِي التَّوْرَاةِ وَالْإِنْجِيلِ
يَأْمُرُهُمْ بِالْمَعْرُوفِ وَيَنْهَاهُمْ عَنِ الْمُنْكَرِ وَيُحِلُّ لَهُمُ الطَّيِّبَاتِ وَيُحَرِّمُ عَلَيْهِمُ الْخَبَائِثَ
وَيَضَعُ عَنْهُمْ إِصْرَهُمْ وَالْأَغْلَالَ الَّتِي كَانَتْ عَلَيْهِمْ ۚ فَالَّذِينَ آمَنُوا بِهِ وَعَزَّرُوهُ وَنَصَرُوهُ
وَاتَّبَعُوا النُّورَ الَّذِي أُنْزِلَ مَعَهُ ۙ أُولَٰئِكَ هُمُ الْمُفْلِحُونَ ۝

"And who follow the Messenger (who is also) the untutored holy Prophet whom they find written in the Tawrah and the Injīl (Bible) with them. He instructs them to do good, prevents them from evil, permits pure things for them, forbids them from impure things and removes from them the burden and shackles that were (binding) upon them. So the successful ones are certainly those who believe in him, honour him, assist him and follow the light (the Qur'ān) revealed with him." (7:157)

Sayyidunā Abū Bakrah reported that the holy Prophet said during pilgrimage:

أَيُّ يَوْمٍ هٰذَا فَسَكَتْنَا حَتّٰى ظَنَنَّا أَنَّهُ سَيُسَمِّيهِ سِوَى اسْمِهِ قَالَ أَلَيْسَ يَوْمَ النَّحْرِ قُلْنَا بَلٰى
قَالَ فَأَيُّ شَهْرٍ هٰذَا فَسَكَتْنَا حَتّٰى ظَنَنَّا أَنَّهُ سَيُسَمِّيهِ بِغَيْرِ اسْمِهِ فَقَالَ أَلَيْسَ بِذِي الْحِجَّةِ
قُلْنَا بَلٰى قَالَ فَإِنَّ دِمَاءَكُمْ وَأَمْوَالَكُمْ وَأَعْرَاضَكُمْ بَيْنَكُمْ حَرَامٌ كَحُرْمَةِ يَوْمِكُمْ هٰذَا فِي
شَهْرِكُمْ هٰذَا فِي بَلَدِكُمْ هٰذَا لِيُبَلِّغِ الشَّاهِدُ الْغَائِبَ فَإِنَّ الشَّاهِدَ عَسٰى أَنْ يُبَلِّغَ مَنْ هُوَ أَوْعٰى
لَهُ مِنْهُ

"What is the day today?" We kept quiet, thinking he might give the day another name. The holy Prophet said, "Is it not the day of sacrificing?" We said, "Yes." The holy Prophet said, "Which month is this?" We again kept quiet thinking he might give it another name. The holy Prophet said, "Is it not the month of Dhul Hijjah?" We said, "Yes." The holy Prophet said, "Verily your lives, your property and your honour are sacred to one another like the sanctity of this day of yours, in this month of yours, in this city of yours. Let one present inform those who were ab-

sent; perhaps one present will inform another who understands better than him." (Bukhārī)

The Hypocrites Would Fake Belief

وَإِذَا لَقُوا الَّذِينَ آمَنُوا قَالُوا آمَنَّا وَإِذَا خَلَوْا إِلَىٰ شَيَاطِينِهِمْ قَالُوا إِنَّا مَعَكُمْ إِنَّمَا نَحْنُ مُسْتَهْزِئُونَ ﴿﴾

"When they meet those who have Īmān (faith) they say, 'We (also) have Īmān!' But when they are alone with their devils (their leaders) they say, 'We are really with you. We were only mocking.'" (2:14)

ذَٰلِكَ بِأَنَّهُمْ آمَنُوا ثُمَّ كَفَرُوا فَطُبِعَ عَلَىٰ قُلُوبِهِمْ فَهُمْ لَا يَفْقَهُونَ ﴿﴾

"This is because they had accepted Īmān (previously) and then committed disbelief, so their hearts were sealed, and they do not understand." (63:3)

In front of the believers, when the hypocrites professed their faith, they were welcomed like believers but their nifāq (hypocrisy) became exposed due to their actions. When a person strays from the Dīn and continually persists in their transgression, Allāh ﷻ seals their heart and when this happens, the call to the path of guidance will fall on deaf ears.

خَتَمَ ٱللَّهُ عَلَىٰ قُلُوبِهِمْ وَعَلَىٰ سَمْعِهِمْ ۖ وَعَلَىٰٓ أَبْصَٰرِهِمْ غِشَٰوَةٌ ۖ وَلَهُمْ عَذَابٌ عَظِيمٌ ۝

"Allāh has placed a seal upon their hearts and upon their hearing, while there is a veil over the eyes. Theirs shall be a terrible punishment." (2:7)

The People of the Book would say that their hearts were sealed:

وَقَالُوا۟ قُلُوبُنَا غُلْفٌۢ ۚ بَل لَّعَنَهُمُ ٱللَّهُ بِكُفْرِهِمْ فَقَلِيلًا مَّا يُؤْمِنُونَ ۝

"They (the Jews mockingly) say, 'Our hearts are covered.' Not at all! Allāh has cursed them because of their disbelief. As a result, there are very few of them who have Imān." (2:88)

In another āyah, Allāh ﷻ says that He will not force it upon those who dislike it:

أَنُلْزِمُكُمُوهَا وَأَنتُمْ لَهَا كَٰرِهُونَ ۝

"Can We force it onto you when you disapprove of it?" (11:28)

In order for a person to be guided, they need to seek guidance. When a person commits a sin, a black spot appears on their heart, this is mentioned in the following hadīth:

Sayyidunā Abū Hurairah رضي الله عنه reported that the Messenger of Allāh ﷺ said:

إِنَّ الْعَبْدَ إِذَا أَخْطَأَ خَطِيئَةً نُكِتَتْ فِي قَلْبِهِ نُكْتَةٌ سَوْدَاءُ فَإِذَا هُوَ نَزَعَ وَاسْتَغْفَرَ وَتَابَ صُقِلَ

قَلْبُهُ وَإِنْ عَادَ زِيدَ فِيهَا حَتَّى تَعْلُوَ قَلْبَهُ وَهُوَ الرَّانُ الَّذِي ذَكَرَ اللَّهُ: (كَلَّا بَلْ رَانَ عَلَى قُلُوبِهِم
مَّا كَانُوا يَكْسِبُونَ)

"Verily when the servant commits a sin, a black mark appears upon his heart. If he abandons the sin, seeks forgiveness and repents, then his heart will be polished. If he returns to the sin, the blackness will be increased until it overcomes his heart. It is the covering that Allāh ﷾ has mentioned: ***Never! In fact, the rust of their sins has covered their hearts."*** **(83:14)** *(Tirmidhī)*

Regarding these people, Allāh ﷾ says:

صُمٌّ بُكْمٌ عُمْيٌ فَهُمْ لَا يَرْجِعُونَ ۝

"Deaf, dumb and blind, they will never return." (2:18)

وَإِذَا رَأَيْتَهُمْ تُعْجِبُكَ أَجْسَامُهُمْ ۖ وَإِن يَقُولُوا تَسْمَعْ لِقَوْلِهِمْ ۖ كَأَنَّهُمْ خُشُبٌ مُّسَنَّدَةٌ ۖ
يَحْسَبُونَ كُلَّ صَيْحَةٍ عَلَيْهِمْ ۚ هُمُ الْعَدُوُّ فَاحْذَرْهُمْ ۚ قَاتَلَهُمُ اللَّهُ ۖ أَنَّىٰ يُؤْفَكُونَ ۝

"When you look at them, their physical appearance appeals to you and when they speak, you listen attentively to what they have to say. They are like sticks leaning against a support. They think that every shout is against them. They are enemies so beware of them. May Allāh destroy them. Where are they wondering astray?" (63:4)

Allāh ﷾ gives the similitude of the hypocrites being as pieces of wood, supported against a wall, like hollow pieces of timber which cannot support itself but has to be propped up against other things. They are devoid of any sincerity and hence are unworthy props to rely on.

'Allāmah Shabbīr Ahmad Uthmāni says: "The wood is dry and lifeless which resembles the Munāfiqūn who are spiritually lifeless. The only thing these pieces of wood can be used for is fire." Timber is generally used for construction work, so the wood which is of no benefit is cast aside and is used as fuel to burn things. In other words, those who feigned belief would only be good for burning.

'Allāmah Jalāluddīn Suyūtī says that this shows this wood is of no benefit, only to be burnt. Just as when the wood piles up and consumes the space in a house which then poses a burden; similarly, the Munāfiqūn are a burden on society.

﴿يَحۡسَبُونَ كُلَّ صَيۡحَةٍ عَلَيۡهِمۡ﴾

"They think that every shout is against them." (63:4)

The hypocrites were always on their guard and cautious about being caught out. So every conversation which was not within their hearing range; they feared that it was a cry against them. They were always apprehensive of their true identity being revealed, which was far from the fine exterior they would attempt to present in order to fool and deceive the believers. This made them secretly probe into prying and eavesdropping on the conversations of the believers in order to monitor their every step and move.

Part of being a believer is that a person leaves that which is of no concern to them as mentioned in the following hadīth:

Sayyidunā Abū Hurairah ﵁ reported that the Messenger of Allāh ﷺ said:

مِنْ حُسْنِ إِسْلَامِ الْمَرْءِ تَرْكُهُ مَا لَا يَعْنِيهِ

"Part of a person being a good Muslim is leaving alone that which does not concern him." (Tirmidhī)

It is forbidden to spy on others as well as backbite. Backbiting should not be a cause of worry for the believers for the sin will be incurred by those who engage in this practice without causing any actual harm to them.

The hypocrites were always anxious because they felt that they had everything to lose if their true identity was to be revealed and made apparent. They did not have the power nor courage to fight the believers openly as disbelievers, so they feigned belief. This in fact made them worse than open enemies.

When a Sūrah was revealed, they would immediately fear that it was about them and that they would be exposed, in thinking that the verses would speak about their hypocrisy:

وَإِذَا مَآ أُنزِلَتْ سُورَةٌ نَّظَرَ بَعْضُهُمْ إِلَىٰ بَعْضٍ ۖ هَلْ يَرَىٰكُم مِّنْ أَحَدٍ ثُمَّ ٱنصَرَفُوا۟ ۚ صَرَفَ ٱللَّهُ

قُلُوبَهُم بِأَنَّهُمْ قَوْمٌ لَّا يَفْقَهُونَ ﴿﴾

"Whenever a Sūrah is revealed, they look at each other (asking by signs), 'Can anyone see you?' Then they turn away. Allāh has turned their hearts away because they are people who have no understanding." (9:127)

هُمُ الْعَدُوُّ فَاحْذَرْهُمْ ۚ قَاتَلَهُمُ اللَّهُ ۖ أَنَّىٰ يُؤْفَكُونَ ﴿﴾

"They are enemies so beware of them. May Allāh destroy them. Where are they wondering astray?" (63:4)

Allāh ﷻ cautioned the holy Prophet ﷺ to be wary of their deceitful tactics in fooling the believers. The holy Prophet ﷺ eventually came to know the identities of all the hypocrites but he kept this information to himself only disclosing this to a few close Companions ﷺ. Everyone is given respite in the world to change and mend their ways and the hypocrites were also given every chance and opportunity to reform themselves. Whatever they would be deserving of in the Ākhirah (Hereafter) would no doubt eventually greet them but for those moments they spent in this worldly life, they had every opportunity to correct and rectify their conduct.

If they had for even a moment contemplated and pondered over the revelation they would have immediately come to the realisation that this had to be divinely inspired for the holy Prophet ﷺ to know their every step and move. Yet instead of acknowledging this, their main concern was the fear of divine revelation being revealed in exposing them.

This indirectly displays that they knew that this message was indeed the truth because they feared their true identity would be disclosed by Allāh ﷻ. Otherwise if they felt that this was not the truth, then after secretly rejecting it why would they have cause to fear that Allāh ﷻ might reveal a verse? Again, this demonstrates the arrogance in their hearts; refusing to believe in the message despite knowing that it was the truth.

Sayyidunā 'Abdullāh ibn Mas'ūd ؓ reported that the holy Prophet ﷺ said:

لَا يَدْخُلُ الْجَنَّةَ مَنْ كَانَ فِيْ قَلْبِهِ مِثْقَالُ ذَرَّةٍ مِّنْ كِبْرٍ فَقَالَ رَجُلٌ إِنَّ الرَّجُلَ يُحِبُّ أَنْ يَّكُوْنَ ثَوْبُهُ حَسَناً وَنَعْلُهُ حَسَنَةً؟ قَالَ: إِنَّ اللهَ جَمِيْلٌ يُحِبُّ الْجَمَالَ الْكِبْرُ بَطَرُ الْحَقِّ وَغَمْطُ النَّاسِ

"No one who has the weight of a seed of arrogance in his heart will enter Paradise." Someone said, "But a man loves to have beautiful clothes and shoes." The holy Prophet ﷺ said, "Verily Allāh is beautiful, and He loves beauty. Arrogance means rejecting the truth and looking down on people." (Muslim)

Allāh ﷻ says:

وَإِذَا قِيْلَ لَهُمْ تَعَالَوْا يَسْتَغْفِرْ لَكُمْ رَسُوْلُ اللهِ لَوَّوْا رُءُوْسَهُمْ وَرَأَيْتَهُمْ يَصُدُّوْنَ وَهُمْ مُّسْتَكْبِرُوْنَ ۞

"When they are told, 'Come forward and Allāh's Messenger will seek forgiveness for you,' they turn their heads around and you see them arrogantly turning away." (63:5)

They had no interest in accepting faith, so gaining the forgiveness of Allāh ﷻ was even far more removed from their hearts.

يَحْذَرُ الْمُنٰفِقُوْنَ اَنْ تُنَزَّلَ عَلَيْهِمْ سُوْرَةٌ تُنَبِّئُهُمْ بِمَا فِىْ قُلُوْبِهِمْ ؕ قُلِ اسْتَهْزِءُوْا ۚ اِنَّ اللّٰهَ مُخْرِجٌ مَّا تَحْذَرُوْنَ ۝

"The hypocrites fear that a Sūrah will be revealed against them, informing them of what is in their hearts. Tell them, 'Mock (as you please)! Surely Allāh will expose that which you fear most'." (9:64)

The true identity of the hypocrites was exposed after the expedition against the Banū Mustaliq. Hārith ibn Abī Dirār, who was the chief of the Jewish tribe of Banū Mustaliq was preparing an army to fight the Muslims according to the historian Muhammad ibn Ishāq. The battle was called Ghazwah Banī Mustaliq. The holy Prophet 's ﷺ army was stationed at a well called al-Muraysī' and it is here that the Banū Mustaliq suffered sound defeat at the hands of the Muslims; the battle took place and the Muslims emerged victorious.

In the battle, Sayyidah Juwayriyah bint Hārith رضي الله عنها who was the daughter of the Banū Mustaliq chief was also captured. Her husband had been killed in the battle. She fell to the lot of Sayyidunā Thābit ibn Qays ibn Shammās رضي الله عنه. Sayyidunā Thābit ibn Qays رضي الله عنه said to her that he was willing to set her free if she gave him a certain amount for her ransom. This was beyond her capacity, so she went to the holy Prophet ﷺ to complain.

She was the daughter of a chieftain and now she had found herself in this plightful condition – how was she to live her life now like a slave? The holy Prophet ﷺ felt pity for her, so after hearing her story, not only did he pay her ransom and free her but also offered to marry her in return, and she accepted this gracious offer.

Subhān-Allāh, this proposal which was put forward was as a result of the holy Prophet's ﷺ foresight and wisdom; for after his marriage to Sayyidah Juwayriyah ﵂, not only did she become one of the wives of the holy Prophet ﷺ and mother of the believers but all the people who were captives of war were all related to her. Hence the people felt embarrassed at holding captive members of the holy Prophet 's ﷺ wife's relatives and as a result, all the prisoners whose numbers reached one hundred households were freed. All the marriages the holy Prophet ﷺ contracted had greater underlying wisdom behind them. It was not just a contract of bringing two people together but securing freedom for entire tribes and communities. Sayyidah 'Ā'ishah ﵂ said that she knew of no other woman who had brought greater blessing to her people than Sayyidah Juwayriyah ﵂.

Those who try to speak about the holy Prophet ﷺ in a disparaging manner, allege that it was because of the beauty of Sayyidah Juwayriyah ﵂ that the holy Prophet ﷺ married her. The holy Prophet 's ﷺ judgement and foresight was remarkable in assessing any given situation and his marriage to Sayyidah Juwayriyah ﵂ paved the way for hundreds of families who gained their freedom from being held as prisoners of war, and this was undoubtedly one of the underlying factors that caused the holy Prophet ﷺ to precede with his proposal of marriage to Sayyidah Juwayriyah رضي الله عنها.

This had already been preordained and destined for the holy Prophet ﷺ as Imām Bayhaqī رحمه الله narrated that Sayyidah Juwayriyah رضي الله عنها said, "Three nights before the battle, I dreamt that the moon appeared from the direction of Yathrib (Madīnah) and fell into my lap, but I decided not to tell anyone about it until the holy Prophet ﷺ arrived. When we were captured, I hoped the dream to come true. There, the holy Prophet ﷺ set me free and then married me." (Ad-Dalā'il)

The Hypocrites See Their Golden Opportunity

After the battle of Banū Mustaliq took place, a Muhājir (migrant) by the name of Jahjāh bin Sa'īd approached an Ansāri man known by the name of Sinān ibn Wabr. A quarrel broke out and the Muhājir man slapped the Ansāri man. The man belonging to the Muhājirūn called out to the Muhājirūn and in like manner, the Ansāri man called out to his tribesmen. This would have almost led to a full-fledged battle had the holy Prophet ﷺ not intervened and calmed down matters. He reminded the people of what had united them in the first place and how they could now deteriorate in their faith and go back to chanting slogans from the days of Jāhiliyyah (ignorance).

The holy Prophet ﷺ upon hearing this said: *"What is this call of Jāhiliyyah? Abandon it because it is offensive."*

The holy Prophet ﷺ came to unite hearts and break down barriers which kept people apart and caused division and now over a petty quarrel, disunity would have emerged within the ranks of the Muslims, had the holy Prophet ﷺ not taken steps to calm the situation. Allāh ﷻ says in the Qur'ān:

يَٰٓأَيُّهَا ٱلنَّاسُ إِنَّا خَلَقْنَٰكُم مِّن ذَكَرٍ وَأُنثَىٰ وَجَعَلْنَٰكُمْ شُعُوبًا وَقَبَآئِلَ لِتَعَارَفُوٓا۟ ۚ إِنَّ أَكْرَمَكُمْ عِندَ ٱللَّهِ أَتْقَىٰكُمْ ۚ إِنَّ ٱللَّهَ عَلِيمٌ خَبِيرٌ ۝

"O people! We have certainly created you from a single male and female, made you into various families and tribes so that you may recognise each other. Verily, the most honoured of you in Allāh's sight is the one with the most taqwā (fear of Allāh). Allāh is certainly All-Knowing, Informed." (49:13)

Sayyidunā 'Abdullāh ibn Umar رضي الله عنه reported that the Messenger of Allāh ﷺ said:

اَلْمُسْلِمُ أَخُو الْمُسْلِمِ، لَا يَظْلِمُهُ وَلَا يُسْلِمُهُ، وَمَنْ كَانَ فِيْ حَاجَةِ أَخِيْهِ كَانَ اللهُ فِيْ حَاجَتِهِ، وَمَنْ فَرَّجَ عَنْ مُسْلِمٍ كُرْبَةً فَرَّجَ اللهُ عَنْهُ كُرْبَةً مِّنْ كُرُبَاتِ يَوْمِ الْقِيَامَةِ، وَمَنْ سَتَرَ مُسْلِمًا سَتَرَهُ اللهُ يَوْمَ الْقِيَامَةِ

"The Muslim is a brother to another Muslim. He does not wrong him nor surrender him. Whoever fulfils the needs of his brother, Allāh will fulfil

his need. Whoever relieves the Muslim from distress, Allāh will relieve him from distress on the Day of Resurrection. Whoever covers the fault of a Muslim, Allāh will cover his faults on the Day of Resurrection." (Bukhārī, Muslim)

Sayyidunā Abū Hurairah ؓ reported that the Messenger of Allāh ﷺ said:

إِنَّ اللهَ لَا يَنْظُرُ إِلَى صُوَرِكُمْ وَأَمْوَالِكُمْ وَلَكِنْ يَنْظُرُ إِلَى قُلُوبِكُمْ وَأَعْمَالِكُمْ

"Verily, Allāh does not look at your appearance or wealth but rather, he looks at your hearts and actions." (Muslim)

Sayyidunā 'Ubādah ibn Sāmit ؓ intervened immediately after hearing the holy Prophet's ﷺ words of admonition and reconciled between the two parties that were quarrelling.

It was at this point that 'Abdullāh ibn 'Ubay saw another golden opportunity and he wasted no time in inciting hatred between the Muhājirūn and Ansār. 'Abdullāh ibn 'Ubay had held a secret consultation and advised against allowing the Muhājirūn to remain in Madīnah saying, "They are bothering us in our land. By Allāh the example of us and the foolish Quraysh men is the example that goes, 'Feed your dog until it becomes strong and it will eat you.'" He also said, "By Allāh when we return to Madīnah, surely the more honourable will expel therefrom the humiliated ones."

Sayyidunā Zayd ibn Arqam ؓ, who was a young boy at the time

heard this and despite being of a tender age, he reprimanded 'Abdullāh ibn 'Ubay. He immediately responded in saying that he had only been joking and he had not meant it, in order to cover his tracks. Sayyidunā Zayd ؓ knew that this was no jesting matter and immediately went to the holy Prophet ﷺ to inform him of the insulting remarks he had heard him say.

The holy Prophet ﷺ called 'Abdullāh ibn 'Ubay and asked him about the matter, to which he replied as to how the holy Prophet ﷺ could possibly believe the word of a child over his word. The holy Prophet ﷺ thought that maybe there had just been a misunderstanding and the child had perhaps not heard correctly. The other hypocrites rallied together in support of 'Abdullāh ibn 'Ubay and so the holy Prophet ﷺ did not press on with the matter any further and let things be.

This led to Sayyidunā Zayd ibn Arqam ؓ to become grief stricken, feeling that he had been labelled a liar. He could not face the holy Prophet ﷺ nor the people but at the same time hoped that revelation would descend in clearing his name.

One day as he stood near the holy Prophet ﷺ, he could see the effects of revelation descending on the holy Prophet ﷺ. The holy Prophet ﷺ then turned to Sayyidunā Zaid ؓ and said, *"O Zayd, Allāh has testified to your words."*

Sayyidunā Ubādah ibn Sāmit ؓ admonished 'Abdullāh ibn 'Ubay

saying that the truth had been revealed and even if he had committed a mistake, he should go to the holy Prophet ﷺ and seek his forgiveness. He reminded him that if the holy Prophet ﷺ did Istighfār (seek forgiveness) for him then he would surely be forgiven. He replied, "You made me believe in him; I have accepted Imān, I have given so much Zakāh, and now you want me to prostrate before him?" This disclosed the hypocrisy he was concealing in his heart which became evident to all the Muslims.

﴿وَإِذَا قِيلَ لَهُمْ تَعَالَوْا إِلَىٰ مَا أَنزَلَ اللَّهُ وَإِلَى الرَّسُولِ رَأَيْتَ الْمُنَافِقِينَ يَصُدُّونَ عَنكَ صُدُودًا﴾

"When it is said to them, 'Come to that which Allāh has revealed and to the Messenger,' you will see the hypocrites turning completely away from you." (4:61)

'Abdullāh ibn 'Ubay's own son, Sayyidunā 'Abdullāh ؓ heard about this and immediately unsheathed his sword waiting at the gate of Madīnah for him to arrive. When he approached, he said to his father, "Stay where you are! By Allāh you will not enter through here until the Messenger of Allāh ﷺ allows you to do so for he is the most honourable one and you are the disgraced." He also said to his father, "You will never enter Madīnah until you say, "Allāh's Messenger is the honourable one and you are the disgraced." Even though he had so much love and respect for his father, he would never tolerate any insult against the holy Prophet ﷺ.

Allāh ﷻ says in the Qur’ān:

لَا تَجِدُ قَوْمًا يُّؤْمِنُوْنَ بِاللّٰهِ وَالْيَوْمِ الْاٰخِرِ يُوَآدُّوْنَ مَنْ حَآدَّ اللّٰهَ وَرَسُوْلَهٗ وَلَوْ كَانُوْٓا اٰبَآءَهُمْ اَوْ
اَبْنَآءَهُمْ اَوْ اِخْوَانَهُمْ اَوْ عَشِيْرَتَهُمْ ؕ اُولٰٓئِكَ كَتَبَ فِيْ قُلُوْبِهِمُ الْاِيْمَانَ وَاَيَّدَهُمْ بِرُوْحٍ مِّنْهُ ؕ
وَيُدْخِلُهُمْ جَنّٰتٍ تَجْرِيْ مِنْ تَحْتِهَا الْاَنْهٰرُ خٰلِدِيْنَ فِيْهَا ؕ رَضِيَ اللّٰهُ عَنْهُمْ وَرَضُوْا عَنْهُ ؕ
اُولٰٓئِكَ حِزْبُ اللّٰهِ ؕ اَلَآ اِنَّ حِزْبَ اللّٰهِ هُمُ الْمُفْلِحُوْنَ ۝

“You will not find people who believe in Allāh and the Last Day befriending those who oppose Allāh and His Messenger even though they are their fathers, their sons, their brothers or their families. These are the people in whose hearts Allāh has written Imān and whom Allāh assists with His mercy. Allāh shall enter them into gardens beneath which rivers flow where they shall live forever. Allāh is pleased with them and they are pleased with Him. They are the group of Allāh. Behold! The group of Allāh shall be the only successful ones.” (58:22)

When Sayyidunā ‘Umar رضي الله عنه heard about this, he asked the holy Prophet ﷺ for permission to behead him. The holy Prophet ﷺ told Sayyidunā ‘Umar رضي الله عنه that this was not the way to go about the matter. He replied by saying, “People will say in that case that Muhammad is killing his own Companions.”

For those who say that Islām allows the killing of those who turn away from Islām, then we should look at the life of the holy Prophet ﷺ and see how he dealt with those people who initially professed faith, but then turned away from faith as Allāh ﷻ described them in this Sūrah. When Sayyidunā 'Umar ﷺ requested permission from the holy Prophet ﷺ to kill 'Abdullāh Ibn 'Ubay, it was not for turning away from Islām but as part of the punishment for treason which we find is universal across the globe.

When the armed forces is out on a military campaign, a person cannot cause disruption and sabotage the forces and anyone who behaves in this manner in the military is considered to have committed an act of treason which is punishable by death in many parts of the world. This was not the time of peace but was a time of high security alert in which this would have had to been dealt with as a crime against the state. Yet even in this situation, the holy Prophet ﷺ chose to overlook and let things be.

Not long after this incident, 'Abdullāh ibn 'Ubay passed away. His son who was also known as 'Abdullāh, requested that the holy Prophet ﷺ lead the Janāzah prayer for his father and also made a special request that his father could be buried in the holy Prophet 's ﷺ garment. Even though his son knew that his father was a Munāfiq, his grief of losing his father had rekindled the feelings of paternal love and it was in this frame of mind that he had made this request. The holy Prophet ﷺ gave his garment for him to be wrapped and buried in.

Sayyidunā 'Umar ﷺ tried to prevent the holy Prophet ﷺ from leading the Janāzah prayer because of all the things that he had said against the holy Prophet ﷺ. The holy Prophet ﷺ then said to Sayyidunā ʻUmar ؓ that Allāh ﷻ had given him a choice, and so he had decided to lead the prayer in asking for forgiveness for him:

سَوَآءٌ عَلَيْهِمْ أَسْتَغْفَرْتَ لَهُمْ أَمْ لَمْ تَسْتَغْفِرْ لَهُمْ ۚ لَن يَغْفِرَ ٱللَّهُ لَهُمْ ۚ إِنَّ ٱللَّهَ لَا يَهْدِي ٱلْقَوْمَ ٱلْفَٰسِقِينَ ۞

"It is the same to them whether you seek forgiveness for them or whether you do not seek forgiveness for them. Allāh shall never forgive them. Verily Allāh does not guide the sinful ones." (63:6)

ٱسْتَغْفِرْ لَهُمْ أَوْ لَا تَسْتَغْفِرْ لَهُمْ ۚ إِن تَسْتَغْفِرْ لَهُمْ سَبْعِينَ مَرَّةً فَلَن يَغْفِرَ ٱللَّهُ لَهُمْ ۚ ذَٰلِكَ بِأَنَّهُمْ كَفَرُوا۟ بِٱللَّهِ وَرَسُولِهِۦ ۗ وَٱللَّهُ لَا يَهْدِى ٱلْقَوْمَ ٱلْفَٰسِقِينَ ۞

"(O Muhammad) seek forgiveness for them or do not seek forgiveness for them. Even if you seek forgiveness for them seventy times, Allāh will never forgive them. That is because they disbelieved in Allāh and His Messenger. Allāh does not guide the disobedient ones." (9:80)

The holy Prophet ﷺ knew that even though he would not be forgiven, he hoped that his tribesmen would perhaps feel inclined to accept Islām in witnessing the holy Prophet's ﷺ love and compassion which he felt for everyone despite their animosity against him.

After the holy Prophet ﷺ had prayed his Janāzah prayer, many of his tribesmen who had initially been against the holy Prophet ﷺ accepted Islām. This action of the holy Prophet ﷺ led to one thousand of his tribe members accepting Islām.

وَلَا تُصَلِّ عَلَىٰٓ أَحَدٍ مِّنْهُم مَّاتَ أَبَدًا وَلَا تَقُمْ عَلَىٰ قَبْرِهِۦٓ ۖ إِنَّهُمْ كَفَرُوا۟ بِٱللَّهِ وَرَسُولِهِۦ وَمَاتُوا۟
وَهُمْ فَٰسِقُونَ ۝

"Do not ever perform (the funeral) Salāh for any of them who die and do not stand over their graves. Undoubtedly they disbelieved in Allāh and His Messenger and died as disobedient people." (9:84)

However, these people had transgressed beyond bounds and therefore it was not befitting for the holy Prophet ﷺ to pray their Janāzah prayer or to stand at their graveside. Allāh ﷻ revealed this verse prohibiting the holy Prophet ﷺ in showing them any form of sorrow or sympathy.

Taking into Consideration the Mindset of the People

The holy Prophet ﷺ wished to reconstruct the Ka'bah and make two doors but because the holy Prophet ﷺ feared initiating a misunderstanding amongst the people in thinking that he was destroying the house of Allāh ﷻ, therefore he left it in its original condition:

Sayyidunā 'Abdullāh ibn Zubayr رضي الله عنه said that he heard Sayyidah

'Ā'ishah ﵂ say that the holy Prophet ﷺ said:

لَوْلَا أَنَّ النَّاسَ حَدِيثٌ عَهْدُهُمْ بِكُفْرٍ وَلَيْسَ عِنْدِي مِنَ النَّفَقَةِ مَا يُقَوِّي عَلَى بِنَائِهِ لَكُنْتُ أَدْخَلْتُ فِيهِ مِنَ الْحِجْرِ خَمْسَةَ أَذْرُعٍ وَجَعَلْتُ لَهُ بَابًا يَدْخُلُ النَّاسُ مِنْهُ وَبَابًا يَخْرُجُونَ مِنْهُ

"If your people had not quite recently abandoned the Ignorance (disbelief) and if I had sufficient provisions to rebuild it (the Ka'bah), I would have added five cubits to it from the Hijr. Also, I would make two doors; one for people to enter therein and the other to exit." (Nasai)

Once, 'Allāmah Shabbīr Ahmad Uthmānī ﵀ was called by the king of Saudi Arabia along with many other scholars from all the different parts of the world. The proposal to break the green dome of Masjid Nabawī was put forward as everyone felt that people were placing too much reverence on the structure.

Everyone agreed to this until 'Allāmah Shabbīr ﵀ spoke using this hadīth as a reference saying that destroying the green dome threatened to place misconceptions in the minds of people who would believe that perhaps the Muslims hated the holy Prophet ﷺ and this is why they had demolished his Masjid. Also, this would cause the Muslims to have hatred for the Saudi government in thinking that they had destroyed such a sacred monument. Immediately, everyone agreed to this and today we still have the green dome in place.

Islām promotes unity and social cohesion. The believers are as one body and one Ummah as the holy Prophet ﷺ said in a hadīth:

مَثَلُ الْمُؤْمِنِيْنَ فِيْ تَوَادِّهِمْ وَتَرَاحُمِهِمْ وَتَعَاطُفِهِمْ مَثَلُ الْجَسَدِ إِذَا اشْتَكَى مِنْهُ عُضْوٌ تَدَاعَى لَهُ سَائِرُ الْجَسَدِ بِالسَّهَرِ وَالْحُمَّى

"The parable of the believers in their affection, compassion and mercy for each other is that of a body. When any limb aches, the whole body reacts with sleeplessness and fever." (Bukhārī)

Punishment for Those Who Spread Evil

إِنَّ الَّذِيْنَ يُحِبُّوْنَ اَنْ تَشِيْعَ الْفَاحِشَةُ فِي الَّذِيْنَ اٰمَنُوْا لَهُمْ عَذَابٌ اَلِيْمٌ فِي الدُّنْيَا وَالْاٰخِرَةِ ۚ وَاللّٰهُ يَعْلَمُ وَاَنْتُمْ لَا تَعْلَمُوْنَ ۞

"There shall be an excruciating punishment in this world and in the hereafter for those who love immorality to spread among the believers. Allāh knows and you do not know." (24:19)

هُمُ الَّذِيْنَ يَقُوْلُوْنَ لَا تُنْفِقُوْا عَلٰى مَنْ عِنْدَ رَسُوْلِ اللّٰهِ حَتّٰى يَنْفَضُّوْا ۚ وَلِلّٰهِ خَزَآئِنُ السَّمٰوٰتِ وَالْاَرْضِ وَلٰكِنَّ الْمُنٰفِقِيْنَ لَا يَفْقَهُوْنَ ۞

"They are the ones who said, 'Do not spend on those with the Messenger of Allāh until they disperse.' To Allāh belongs the treasures of the heavens and the earth but the hypocrites do not

understand." **(63:7)**

'Abdullāh ibn 'Ubay incited the Ansār into believing that the Muhājirūn whom they had provided a haven for, would eventually overtake their land and city. He misled them into thinking that they had helped them after they had been bereft of any financial means and now, they were ungrateful and showing their ingratitude. Allāh ﷻ is reminding them in this verse that even the wealth which we have at our disposal, even this is not ours, but everything belongs to Allāh ﷻ, and ultimately we will all be returned to Him.

For example, people come to the local masājid to collect sadaqah but the people are reluctant to give or give in a miserly manner. Sayyidunā Abū Hurairah رضي الله عنه reported that the Messenger of Allāh ﷺ said:

مَا نَقَصَتْ صَدَقَةٌ مِنْ مَالٍ وَمَا زَادَ اللهُ عَبْدًا بِعَفْوٍ إِلَّا عِزًّا وَمَا تَوَاضَعَ أَحَدٌ لِلّٰهِ إِلَّا رَفَعَهُ اللهُ

"Charity does not decrease wealth, no one forgives another but that Allāh increases his honour, and no one humbles himself for the sake of Allāh, but that Allāh raises his status." (Muslim)

A person for example, may come all the way from a different country in collecting donations. We should feel honoured to be able to give to these people because we could not have gone all the way to these places personally providing it to the people.. We should feel fortunate that they have come to us so that we can have the honour of reaping such great rewards in providing for them.

Only Allāh ﷻ has the treasures of the heavens and the earth. The Munāfiqūn felt that if they stopped giving to the Muslims, then they would be left poverty stricken and would have been forced to retreat and go back to where they came from.

مَثَلُ الَّذِينَ يُنفِقُونَ أَمْوَالَهُمْ فِي سَبِيلِ اللَّهِ كَمَثَلِ حَبَّةٍ أَنبَتَتْ سَبْعَ سَنَابِلَ فِي كُلِّ سُنبُلَةٍ مِّائَةُ حَبَّةٍ ۗ وَاللَّهُ يُضَاعِفُ لِمَن يَشَاءُ ۗ وَاللَّهُ وَاسِعٌ عَلِيمٌ ۝

"The likeness of those who spend in the way of Allāh is like a grain which grows seven ears, in every ear (there are) a hundred grains. Allāh increases for those whom He Wills. Allāh is All-Embracing, All-Knowing." (2:261)

يَقُولُونَ لَئِن رَّجَعْنَا إِلَى الْمَدِينَةِ لَيُخْرِجَنَّ الْأَعَزُّ مِنْهَا الْأَذَلَّ ۚ وَلِلَّهِ الْعِزَّةُ وَلِرَسُولِهِ وَلِلْمُؤْمِنِينَ وَلَٰكِنَّ الْمُنَافِقِينَ لَا يَعْلَمُونَ ۝

They say, 'If we return to Madīnah , the honourable ones among us shall certainly exile the humiliated ones. All honour belongs to Allāh, His Messenger and the believers but the Munāfiqūn do not know it." (63:8)

'Abdullāh ibn 'Ubay thought of himself as the respected one and referred to the Messenger of Allāh ﷺ and the Muslims as the humiliated ones. Allāh ﷻ is saying that honour lies with Allāh ﷻ, His Messenger ﷺ and the true believers even though the Munāfiqūn refused to acknowledge this.

As the world echoes the name of the holy Prophet ﷺ and his noble

Companions ﷺ from the four corners of the globe, we come to realise the great position of honour and esteem Allāh ﷻ has given the holy Prophet ﷺ and his faithful Companions as billions of people honour and follow them as their role models.

The hypocrites on the other hand, not only suffered disgrace when their true identifies were revealed, but will be remembered with contempt by all the believers who will come until the Day of Judgement. The hypocrites are referred to as 'Lā Yafqahūn (do not understand) in a previous verse and in this verse, the Arabic word 'La Ya'lamūn' (do not know) is used. The reason for the subtle difference is that the hypocrites felt they were the providers of the believers. This idea had to be dispelled in informing them that these treasures were not in their hands to do as they pleased. This wealth has been assigned to certain individuals so that they dispose of it in the correct manner according to the Book of Allāh ﷻ.

Some people feel that they are worthy of respect because of the great wealth in their hands forgetting that it is Allāh ﷻ Who has given them this and it is He who gives dignity and respect to whomever He wishes to honour.

Allāh ﷻ constrains the wealth for some and expands for others, His authority extends over the heavens and the earth and He has the power to do as He wishes. Even in the worldly life, people who are wealthy generally have a high status and position and are held in high esteem, but if they have not disposed their wealth in the correct manner, then this will only be a burden for them on the Day of Judgement and their riches will not avail them against Allāh's wrath and anger.

Sa'īd ibn Musayyib, the great Tābi'ī said that once a black slave came to him and felt a little reluctant to speak as a result of feeling inferior in front of the Arabs. Sa'īd ibn Musayyib said to him, "O my brother, do not be afraid to speak because you are black in complexion. The best of all three people were black." These three great people were:

1. Sayyidunā Bilāl
2. Sayyidunā Luqmān
3. Sayyidunā Mahjāh

Regarding Sayyidunā Bilāl, the holy Prophet asked him as to what deed he had carried out for he had heard his footsteps in front of him in Paradise. Sayyidunā Abū Hurairah narrated:

أَنَّ النَّبِيَّ صَلَّى اللهُ عَلَيْهِ وَسَلَّمَ قَالَ لِبِلَالٍ عِنْدَ صَلَاةِ الْفَجْرِ "يَا بِلَالُ حَدِّثْنِي بِأَرْجَى عَمَلٍ عَمِلْتَهُ فِي الْإِسْلَامِ، فَإِنِّي سَمِعْتُ دَفَّ نَعْلَيْكَ بَيْنَ يَدَيَّ فِي الْجَنَّةِ". قَالَ مَا عَمِلْتُ عَمَلًا أَرْجَى عِنْدِي أَنِّي لَمْ أَتَطَهَّرْ طُهُورًا فِي سَاعَةِ لَيْلٍ أَوْ نَهَارٍ إِلَّا صَلَّيْتُ بِذَلِكَ الطُّهُورِ مَا كُتِبَ لِي أَنْ أُصَلِّيَ

At the time of Fajr prayer the holy Prophet asked Bilāl, "Tell me of the best deed that you did after embracing Islām, for I heard your footsteps in front of me in Paradise." Bilāl replied, "I did not do anything worth mentioning except that when I performed ablution during the day or night I prayed after that ablution as much as was written for me." (Bukhārī)

وَلَقَدْ آتَيْنَا لُقْمَانَ الْحِكْمَةَ أَنِ اشْكُرْ لِلَّهِ ۚ وَمَن يَشْكُرْ فَإِنَّمَا يَشْكُرُ لِنَفْسِهِ ۖ وَمَن كَفَرَ فَإِنَّ اللَّهَ غَنِيٌّ حَمِيدٌ ۝

"We certainly granted wisdom to Luqmān (inspiring him) to express gratitude to Allāh. Whoever is grateful to Allāh, expresses gratitude for his own benefit. As for him who is ungrateful, Allāh is certainly Independent, Most Worthy of praise." (31:12)

Wahb ibn Munabbīh said, "I have read 10,000 words of wisdom of Sayyidunā Luqmān.

Sayyidunā Mahjāh was the slave of Sayyidunā 'Umar who reached a high position and status of becoming one of the greatest scholars of his time.

Nowhere more is this unity visible than when a person goes for hajj. Two sheets of cloth is all that is worn and wrapped around a person's body so that there remains no difference between one person from another; regardless of whether they are rich or poor; everyone stands here on the same plain, dressed in the same clothes and chanting the same praise of Allāh in the same manner regardless of their ethnicity, colour or race. Everyone stands united in one single brotherhood.

This airs a feeling of a sense of invincibility when we cast our minds back to the time when Sayyidunā Khālid ibn Walīd ﷺ had come to attack the Muslims and destroy them as they set off for Umrah, donned in their Ihrām with no weapons to defend themselves except their traveller's swords. Yet despite trying to provoke them, the Muslims stood their ground and Sayyidunā Khālid ibn Walīd ﷺ and his men were unable to harm them. This unity and brotherhood undoubtedly left a deep impression in the mind of Sayyidunā Khālid ibn Walīd ﷺ who later went on to accept Islām and become one of the greatest warrior that the world had ever witnessed.

A person who is deeply loved will also undoubtedly have those who are jealous and envious and are on the other side of the spectrum. So long as we stay true to our pledge and follow the Dīn then we should not feel anxious or agonise about what others think of us.

The holy Prophet ﷺ said that the best type of hajj is where the most Talbiyah is recited and a person makes a sacrifice of an animal.

Sayyidunā Abū Hurairah ﷺ reported that the Messenger of Allāh ﷺ said, *"A pilgrim never raises his voice answering the call of Allāh (Talbiyah) but that he is given glad tidings, and a pilgrim never raises his voice in exalting Allāh (Takbīr) but that he is given glad tidings." It was said, "O Messenger of Allāh, of Paradise?" The holy Prophet ﷺ said, "Yes."*

We have the five times daily prayers which should also be performed in congregation, thus highlighting the importance of solidarity and the unification of people being united together under one banner.

The Jumu'ah prayer also unites all the people every week in making this day the most auspicious day of the week. The two Eids are the yearly gatherings which bring the people together, and the universal gathering to the House of Allāh is once in a lifetime for those who have the financial means to do so.

Take Your Own Advice

Once a father and son set off on a journey and had both decided to travel sitting on one donkey. As they passed by a group of people, the people called out, "What are you doing, you are going to kill the poor donkey!" Upon hearing this, they both climbed down from the donkey and continued with the journey on foot. Moments later, they met another group of people who approached them and said, "What is the point of having a donkey when none of you are sat upon it?" Upon hearing this, the son mounted on the donkey and the father walked on.

A little while later, they then came upon another group of people who were remarking amongst themselves, "Look at the youth of nowadays! The poor old father is walking whilst the son gets to ride on the donkey." The father upon hearing this told his son that he would get on the donkey and ride on it instead.

After they travelled further, they met another group of people who after seeing them began to say, "Look at that poor son with sweat pouring from his face whilst the father rides in comfort." The father then got off the donkey and thought of what he should do next. The father and son decided to tie the donkey to a pole and carry it instead. They came across a bridge which they had to cross. The donkey accidentally slipped from their hands and fell straight into the water. The father then looked at the son and said, "Next time we will just please ourselves."

We will never manage to satisfy everyone despite how hard we try and at times this becomes a source of grief which causes depression amongst many individuals. We must remember that so long as we are doing those actions which are pleasing to Allāh ﷻ, then everything else should be of no concern and losing sleep over.

The Munāfiqūn would always cause problems for the holy Prophet ﷺ but he would overlook them, time and time again. However, anything they heard from the holy Prophet ﷺ, they would immediately find fault and criticise in portraying the holy Prophet ﷺ in a negative light.

إِنَّ الَّذِيْنَ كَفَرُوْا سَوَآءٌ عَلَيْهِمْ ءَاَنْذَرْتَهُمْ اَمْ لَمْ تُنْذِرْهُمْ لَا يُؤْمِنُوْنَ۞

"Verily, it makes no difference to the disbelievers whether you warn them or do not warn them; they will still not have īmān (faith)." (2:6)

The Arabic word 'Sawāun 'Alayhim' (upon them) is used which means that even if the person invited to Islām does not accept or believe, the person giving the Da'wah will continue to be rewarded for their efforts each time they call them to accept Islām, despite the fact that the person may continue to reject and never go on to accept Īmān.

Once when there was torrential rain, Abū Jahl was sat with his wife at home and proclaimed, "If Muhammad was to come knocking on my door at this moment and request me to accept Islām, I would accept. Almost immediately, there was a knock at the door and when Abū Jahl went to open the door, he found the holy Prophet ﷺ standing there. The holy Prophet ﷺ invited him to accept the message, but he refused and slammed the door.

Another time, Abū Jahl had a stone in his hand and he said to the holy Prophet ﷺ, "O Muhammad, if you can tell me what is in my hand then I will accept Islām". The holy Prophet ﷺ said, "What if the stone tells you who I am, will you accept?" The stone then miraculously spoke, "I give witness that you are the Messenger of Allāh ﷺ." Abū Jahl claimed that this was the work of sorcery and witch-craft and hence he refused to accept.
The lesson which we derive from this is that the effort is from us, but the completion is from Allāh ﷻ. For example, Sayyidunā Nūh عليه السلام preached to his people for 950 years to accept his message:

وَلَقَدْ أَرْسَلْنَا نُوحًا إِلَىٰ قَوْمِهِ فَلَبِثَ فِيهِمْ أَلْفَ سَنَةٍ إِلَّا خَمْسِينَ عَامًا ۖ فَأَخَذَهُمُ الطُّوفَانُ

وَهُمْ ظٰلِمُوْنَ ۞

“Without doubt We sent Nūh to his nation, where he remained for a thousand years less fifty years (950 years). Then a storm struck them while they were oppressive.” (29:14)

The Mufassirūn (interpreters of the Qur’ān) mention that despite this great length of time preaching, only about 80 people accepted his message, that is equivalent to one person every 12 years. When the holy Prophet ﷺ went on the journey of Mi’rāj, he saw a prophet with a large group of followers, he then saw a prophet with one follower, followed by a prophet who did not have a single follower, but his (this prophet’s) status is greater than all the people put together because of the effort he had made.

يٰٓاَيُّهَا الَّذِيْنَ اٰمَنُوْا لَا تُلْهِكُمْ اَمْوَالُكُمْ وَلَآ اَوْلَادُكُمْ عَنْ ذِكْرِ اللّٰهِ ۚ وَمَنْ يَّفْعَلْ ذٰلِكَ فَاُولٰٓئِكَ هُمُ الْخٰسِرُوْنَ ۞

“O you who have īmān! Let not your wealth and your children make you neglect Allāh’s remembrance. Those who do this are certainly losers.” (63:9)

In this verse, Allāh ﷻ gives us the remedy from falling into hypocrisy. Many a times, we are so absorbed and engaged in accumulating for our worldly needs that our concern for the Hereafter is neglected. During the time of the holy Prophet ﷺ, the people would derive the greatest pleasure in their accumulation of their wealth and having a large number of children which gave them a sense of a feeling of power and invincibility. They felt that their pride came from their wealth and lineage and depended upon their sons in taking over their affairs after them.

A present-day example of this would be regarding some parents who show arrogance in boasting about their children studying a certain degree or doctorate and compare it to another person's child in feeling that their child is at a higher standard and rank. Wealth and children are used as a symbol of status and many a times, a person feels that their honour and prestige lie within these things and so they end up spending all of their endeavour and effort in directing it into those things whilst neglecting their real sense of purpose.

When a person remembers Allāh ﷻ, they call to mind Allāh's ﷻ grandeur and majesty and do not lose sight of their own meek status in comparison to His greatness. The increasing remembrance of Allāh ﷻ as our Master and we as His servants is the remedy which causes a person to increase in humbleness. If the dhikr of Allāh ﷻ fails to dispel the arrogance within a person's heart, then this person is far away from Allāh ﷻ and they will be amongst the ultimate losers in the hereafter.

This world is not a place to hoard things and Allāh ﷻ says in this āyah to spend and give in the path of Allāh ﷻ, before a day will come when a person will hope that they could give everything in the path of Allāh ﷻ but by this time it will be too late.

The word Infāq (spending) comes from the same origin as nifāq (hypocrisy). In this verse, Allāh ﷻ is saying that spending in the path of Allāh ﷻ is the actual antidote for nifāq (hypocrisy). When a person is charitable, then this accumulates good deeds for the person in the Hereafter which is the opposite of a hypocrite who only wishes to cling on to worldly assets and possessions. Infāq will extinguish nifāq because when a person hoards their wealth, they feel they are worth something more than they actually are and this is the essence of hypocrisy.

In another verse, Allāh ﷻ gives examples directly addressing the Munāfiqūn of the nations that were destroyed as a result of rejecting the message:

كَالَّذِينَ مِنْ قَبْلِكُمْ كَانُوٓا أَشَدَّ مِنْكُمْ قُوَّةً وَّأَكْثَرَ أَمْوَالًا وَّأَوْلَادًا ۖ فَاسْتَمْتَعُوا بِخَلَاقِهِمْ
فَاسْتَمْتَعْتُمْ بِخَلَاقِكُمْ كَمَا اسْتَمْتَعَ الَّذِينَ مِنْ قَبْلِكُمْ بِخَلَاقِهِمْ وَخُضْتُمْ كَالَّذِي خَاضُوٓا ۖ
أُولَٰٓئِكَ حَبِطَتْ أَعْمَالُهُمْ فِي الدُّنْيَا وَالْاٰخِرَةِ ۚ وَأُولَٰٓئِكَ هُمُ الْخٰسِرُونَ ۝

"(O Munāfiqūn, you are) just like those before you. They were more powerful than you and possessed more wealth and children than you. They enjoyed their share (of this world) and you enjoyed your share just as those before you enjoyed theirs. You indulged (in evil) just as those who indulged. It was they whose actions were destroyed in this world and in the Hereafter. It is they who are the losers." (9:69)

Allāh ﷻ then warns the Munāfiqūn addressing them about the former nations who were destroyed:

أَلَمْ يَأْتِهِمْ نَبَأُ الَّذِينَ مِن قَبْلِهِمْ قَوْمِ نُوحٍ وَعَادٍ وَثَمُودَ وَقَوْمِ إِبْرَاهِيمَ وَأَصْحَابِ مَدْيَنَ وَالْمُؤْتَفِكَاتِ ۚ أَتَتْهُمْ رُسُلُهُم بِالْبَيِّنَاتِ ۖ فَمَا كَانَ اللَّهُ لِيَظْلِمَهُمْ وَلَٰكِن كَانُوا أَنفُسَهُمْ يَظْلِمُونَ ۞

"Did the news of those before them not reach them, the nation of Nūh, 'Ād, Thamūd, the people of Ibrāhīm, the inhabitants of Madyan and the overturned cities? Their messengers came to them with clear proofs. It is not (possible) for Allāh to oppress them, but they oppressed themselves." (9:70)

The inner greed of the fear of losing their wealth to the Muslims is what kept the Munāfiqūn away from accepting Islām and continuing feigning belief. It is narrated in Ibn Mājah:

جَاءَ الْحَسَنُ وَالْحُسَيْنُ يَسْعَيَانِ إِلَى النَّبِيِّ صَلَّى اللهُ عَلَيْهِ وَسَلَّمَ فَضَمَّهُمَا إِلَيْهِ وَقَالَ إِنَّ الْوَلَدَ مَبْخَلَةٌ مَجْبَنَةٌ

"Hasan and Husain came running to the holy Prophet ﷺ and he embraced them both and said, 'Children make a man a miser and a coward'." (Ibn Mājah)

In an attempt to save all their wealth for their children, they seize spending their money and thus this makes a person miserly. Also, if they go on to fight in the path of Allāh ﷻ and are killed, they feel that their children will be left abandoned and will have no one to look after them. There are those who even defer carrying out hajj in fear of suffering from for example, an accident or a plane crash etc.

Family Responsibility

To support and provide for the family is compulsory for a man. Every person is responsible for those under their care. Sayyidunā 'Abdullāh ibn 'Umar ﷺ reported that the Messenger of Allāh ﷺ said:

أَلَا كُلُّكُمْ رَاعٍ وَكُلُّكُمْ مَسْئُوْلٌ عَنْ رَعِيَّتِهِ، فَالْإِمَامُ الَّذِيْ عَلَى النَّاسِ رَاعٍ وَهُوَ مَسْئُوْلٌ عَنْ رَعِيَّتِهِ، وَالرَّجُلُ رَاعٍ عَلَى أَهْلِ بَيْتِهِ وَهُوَ مَسْئُوْلٌ عَنْ رَعِيَّتِهِ، وَالْمَرْأَةُ رَاعِيَةٌ عَلَى أَهْلِ بَيْتِ زَوْجِهَا وَوَلَدِهِ وَهِيَ مَسْئُوْلَةٌ عَنْهُمْ، وَعَبْدُ الرَّجُلِ رَاعٍ عَلَى مَالِ سَيِّدِهِ وَهُوَ مَسْئُوْلٌ عَنْهُ، أَلَا فَكُلُّكُمْ رَاعٍ وَكُلُّكُمْ مَسْئُوْلٌ عَنْ رَعِيَّتِهِ

"Every one of you is a shepherd and is responsible for his flock. The leader of people is a guardian and is responsible for his subjects. A man is the guardian of his family and he is responsible for them. A woman is the guardian of her husband's home and his children and she is responsible for them. The servant of a man is a guardian of the property of his master and he is responsible for it. No doubt, every one of you is a shepherd and is responsible for his flock." (Bukhārī, Muslim)

It is obligatory to earn a livelihood for that amount which is sufficient. If a person works day and night and forgets the true purpose of life, then what could be of a greater loss? Our Shaykh once met a

man who worked nearly 18 hours a day. His objective was that as he had five children, he wished to purchase five freehold houses for his five children. He would survive on a sandwich and a coke which was his ration of food in order to save the rest of the money.
Allāh ﷻ says in the Qur'ān:

وَاعْبُدْ رَبَّكَ حَتَّىٰ يَأْتِيَكَ الْيَقِينُ ۝

"And worship your Lord until the certainty (death) comes to you. (15:99)

The Arabic word dhikr which is used in this verse refers to all the different types of worship in calling to mind Allāh's remembrance.

وَأَنفِقُوا مِن مَّا رَزَقْنَاكُم مِّن قَبْلِ أَن يَأْتِيَ أَحَدَكُمُ الْمَوْتُ فَيَقُولَ رَبِّ لَوْلَا أَخَّرْتَنِي إِلَىٰ أَجَلٍ قَرِيبٍ فَأَصَّدَّقَ وَأَكُن مِّنَ الصَّالِحِينَ ۝

"Spend from what We have provided for you before death comes to any of you and then he says, 'O my Lord! Why do you not grant me respite for a little while longer so that I can spend in charity and become of the righteous'." (63:10)

Sayyidunā 'Alī ؓ said, "The dunya (worldly life) is going away from you and the Ākhirah (Hereafter) is coming towards you. And for each of these places there are people. So, become people of the Ākhirah and do not become people of the dunya. Today is the time for 'amal (deeds), there is no hisāb (reckoning). Tomorrow there will be hisāb and no chance to do the 'amal."

When the holy Prophet ﷺ was asked what kind of Ṣadaqah is best, he replied giving in the path of Allāh ﷻ whilst you have the greed for it. Sayyidunā Abū Hurairah رضي الله عنه reported:

جَاءَ رَجُلٌ إِلَى النَّبِيِّ صَلَّى اللهُ عَلَيْهِ وَسَلَّمَ فَقَالَ يَا رَسُولَ اللهِ أَيُّ الصَّدَقَةِ أَعْظَمُ أَجْرًا فَقَالَ أَنْ تَصَدَّقَ وَأَنْتَ صَحِيحٌ شَحِيحٌ تَخْشَى الْفَقْرَ وَتَأْمُلُ الْغِنَاءَ وَلَا تُمْهِلُ حَتَّى إِذَا بَلَغَتِ الْحُلْقُومَ قُلْتَ لِفُلَانٍ كَذَا وَلِفُلَانٍ كَذَا وَقَدْ كَانَ لِفُلَانٍ

"A man came to the holy Prophet ﷺ and he said, "O Messenger of Allāh, which charity has the greatest reward?" The holy Prophet ﷺ said, "That you give charity while you are healthy, feeling greedy, fearing poverty, and hoping to be rich. Do not delay giving until you are on your deathbed, then say give such and such a person. It already belongs to that person." (Bukhārī)

Allāh ﷻ says:

أَلْهَٰكُمُ التَّكَاثُرُ ۝ حَتَّىٰ زُرْتُمُ الْمَقَابِرَ ۝

"Rivalry in amassing wealth has made you negligent until you reach the graves." (102:1-2)

On one headstone it was written, "O you who is standing in front of my grave, do not be astonished at my condition, for yesterday I was like you and tomorrow you will be like me."

﴿رَبِّ لَوْلَآ أَخَّرْتَنِيٓ إِلَىٰٓ أَجَلٖ قَرِيبٖ فَأَصَّدَّقَ﴾

"O my Lord! Why do you not grant me respite for a little while longer so that I can spend in charity" (63:10)

The scholars of tafsīr mention that here it refers to a person who will not ask for a great length of time; just long enough to discharge their sadaqah and all the wealth that was due on them.

﴿وَأَكُن مِّنَ ٱلصَّٰلِحِينَ﴾

"And become of the righteous." (63:10)

Sayyidunā 'Abdullāh ibn 'Abbās ﷺ says that this refers to a person who had not preformed their Hajj which was obligatory on them. So, they will ask Allāh ﷻ to allow them to perform hajj so that they can be from amongst the righteous.

At this time, when those who are destined for the Hellfire will be driven to their destination, they will be regretting and crying out in pain and agony pleading with Allāh ﷻ to allow them to return so that they could carry out good deeds. Allāh ﷻ says in the Qur'ān:

﴿وَلَن يُؤَخِّرَ ٱللَّهُ نَفْسًا إِذَا جَآءَ أَجَلُهَا ۚ وَٱللَّهُ خَبِيرُۢ بِمَا تَعْمَلُونَ﴾

"Allāh shall not grant respite to any soul when its term arrives. Allāh is Informed of what you do." (63:11)

When we recite the following verse when a person dies:

إِنَّا لِلَّهِ وَإِنَّا إِلَيْهِ رَاجِعُونَ ۝

"Verily we belong to Allāh and to Him shall we return." (2:156)

We are reaffirming that just as this person has returned to Allāh ﷻ, we too will have to return back to Him one day. Allāh ﷻ is Mālik (Sovereign) and we are His mamlūk (servants). The people who pass away will never be returned to us. If we wish to be re-united with our loved ones, then we need to carry out righteous deeds and actions so that we can be reunited with all of those who were beloved to ourselves and Allāh ﷻ in the next world and not in this world.

On the Day of Judgement, a person will beg to be given a few moments so that they could give everything in Sadaqah:

حَتَّىٰٓ إِذَا جَآءَ أَحَدَهُمُ ٱلْمَوْتُ قَالَ رَبِّ ٱرْجِعُونِ ﴿٩٩﴾ لَعَلِّيٓ أَعْمَلُ صَٰلِحًا فِيمَا تَرَكْتُ ۚ كَلَّآ ۚ إِنَّهَا كَلِمَةٌ هُوَ قَآئِلُهَا ۖ وَمِن وَرَآئِهِم بَرْزَخٌ إِلَىٰ يَوْمِ يُبْعَثُونَ ﴿١٠٠﴾

"Until the time arrives when death comes to any one of them, then he says, 'O my Lord! Allow me to return so that I may perform good deeds in that (worldly life) which I have left behind.' Never! It is merely a statement that they speak. Behind them is barzakh (a barrier) until the day that they are resurrected." (23:99-100)

Allāh ﷻ will remind the person that they were given enough time to seek admonition:

وَهُمْ يَصْطَرِخُونَ فِيهَا ۚ رَبَّنَآ أَخْرِجْنَا نَعْمَلْ صَٰلِحًا غَيْرَ ٱلَّذِى كُنَّا نَعْمَلُ ۚ أَوَلَمْ نُعَمِّرْكُم مَّا يَتَذَكَّرُ فِيهِ مَن تَذَكَّرَ وَجَآءَكُمُ ٱلنَّذِيرُ ۖ فَذُوقُوا۟ فَمَا لِلظَّٰلِمِينَ مِن نَّصِيرٍ

"The disbelievers will be screaming in Jahannam saying, 'Our Lord! Remove us from here and we will do deeds unlike those that we used to carry out.' (It will be said to them), 'Did we not grant you sufficient age (time) in which the one who takes heed may take heed? And did a warner not come to you? So, taste (the punishment for your wrongdoing)!' The oppressors will not have a helper." (35:37)

A 'warner' refers to the holy Prophet ﷺ. Scholars of tafsīr have mentioned that a 'warner' also refers to our own life. When a person progresses through the different stages of their life, this is an indirect warning that they are approaching closer to their death. For example, a person gets married, has children, has grandchildren etc.

Once a person saw Izrā'īl عليه السلام in their dream and said to him, "You are strange. You just come suddenly and take the rūḥ (soul) of a person, why do you not give a reminder?" Izrā'īl عليه السلام said in the dream, "I give you so many reminders. Your marriage is a reminder, your grey hair is a reminder, your grandchildren are all reminders."

When we are stricken with an illness, this is also an admonition that our health will eventually deteriorate and will not last forever. Every day, we see and hear of many people dying, some who are very beloved and close to us, and these are all things that make us recall the remembrance of death.

From this āyah, we can conclude that giving sadaqah is one of the best deeds because at that moment, a person will wish for this opportunity. Giving sadaqah will save a person from a terrible death. We should make the intention that every week, we will donate to the Masjid, or to the orphans and needy, or any noble cause which will earn reward for us. Allāh ﷻ will not delay for even a fraction of a moment when the time of death is decreed for a person.

Hakīmul Ummah Shaykh Ashraf 'Alī Thānwi ؒ says, "To have children is a blessing and not to have children is also a blessing. He himself, despite having two wives had no children. He wrote over a thousand books and he said that Allāh ﷻ had allowed him to accomplish all this which perhaps would not been possible if he had children to tend to. If a person was to count the number of pages in his books, they outnumber the days of his life. He lived for over 80 years.

Once when Shaykh Abul Hasan 'Ali Nadwī ؒ was giving a lecture in front of the Arabs, he was saying, "Can you show me any scholar in the last century who has written more pages than the number of days of his life?" Everyone remained silent. Shaykh Nadwī ؒ spoke again saying, "I will mention one name – Hakīmul Ummah Shaykh Ashraf 'Alī Thānwī." His books have been printed across the globe in various languages.

Shaykh Zakariyya Kāndhlawī was also a prominent Shaykh who left behind lasting impressions such as his book Fadā'il 'A'māl which is read by millions. It is said that there is no moment of the day or night that Fadā'il 'A'māl is not read because in some parts of the world when it is the hours of darkness, it is the hours of daylight in other parts.

If a person has children who are pious and make du'ā for their parents, then these parents are fortunate. On the other hand, if we raise children who are disobedient because we have failed to bring them up in the proper manner, then this will be the cause of great difficulty on the Day of Judgement and for some their children will even take them to the fire of Jahannam. May Allāh protect us all from such a fate!

There will be those who will protest to Allāh that they were not taught the teachings and beliefs by those whose care they were entrusted under. Therefore, a woman for example, may take the following male members of her family to the Hellfire if they fail in their duty:

1. Her father
2. Her son
3. Her brother
4. Her husband

وَقَالَ الَّذِينَ كَفَرُوا رَبَّنَآ أَرِنَا الَّذَيْنِ أَضَلَّانَا مِنَ الْجِنِّ وَالْإِنسِ نَجْعَلْهُمَا تَحْتَ أَقْدَامِنَا لِيَكُونَا مِنَ الْأَسْفَلِينَ ۞

"Those who commit disbelief will say, 'O our Lord! Show us the two groups from the Jinn and humankind who misled us. We want to trample them beneath our feet so that they become of those who are most humiliated'." (41:29)

The disbelievers, when they see their eternal fate of misery will wish to sever all connections with even those who were most closet and dearest to them in the world, who were the reason for their misguidance. They will wish to crush those who misled them and ask Allāh ﷻ to be given a chance.

We must act now whilst we still have the chance to do so; in making every moment count in obeying Allāh ﷻ and following His commands before a day comes when regret will be of no benefit.

May Allāh ﷻ keep our hearts free from jealousy and hypocrisy and allow us to spend in His path; in saving us from being miserly and the desire to cling on to the deceptive treasures of this worldly life, Āmīn.

بسم الله الرحمن الرحيم

English Translation of

سورة المنٰفقون

Sūrah 63 Al Munāfiqūn (The Hypocrites)

(Madani | 11 Verses)

When the Munāfiqūn come to you they say, 'We testify that you are certainly Allāh's Messenger.' Allāh knows well that you are His Messenger and Allāh testifies that the Munāfiqūn are liars.	1	إِذَا جَآءَكَ الْمُنٰفِقُوْنَ قَالُوْا نَشْهَدُ إِنَّكَ لَرَسُوْلُ اللّٰهِ ۘ وَاللّٰهُ يَعْلَمُ إِنَّكَ لَرَسُوْلُهٗ ؕ وَاللّٰهُ يَشْهَدُ إِنَّ الْمُنٰفِقِيْنَ لَكٰذِبُوْنَ
They use their oaths as shields and prevent (others) from Allāh's path. Evil indeed is that which they do.	2	اِتَّخَذُوْٓا أَيْمَانَهُمْ جُنَّةً فَصَدُّوْا عَنْ سَبِيْلِ اللّٰهِ ؕ إِنَّهُمْ سَآءَ مَا كَانُوْا يَعْمَلُوْنَ
This is because they had accepted īmān (previously) and then committed disbelief, so their hearts were sealed, and they do not understand.	3	ذٰلِكَ بِأَنَّهُمْ اٰمَنُوْا ثُمَّ كَفَرُوْا فَطُبِعَ عَلٰى قُلُوْبِهِمْ فَهُمْ لَا يَفْقَهُوْنَ
When you look at them, their physical appearance appeals to you and when they speak, you listen attentively to what they have to say. They are like sticks leaning against a support. They think that every shout is against them. They are enemies so beware of them. May Allāh destroy them. Where are they wondering astray?	4	وَإِذَا رَأَيْتَهُمْ تُعْجِبُكَ أَجْسَامُهُمْ ؕ وَإِنْ يَّقُوْلُوْا تَسْمَعْ لِقَوْلِهِمْ ؕ كَأَنَّهُمْ خُشُبٌ مُّسَنَّدَةٌ ؕ يَحْسَبُوْنَ كُلَّ صَيْحَةٍ عَلَيْهِمْ ؕ هُمُ الْعَدُوُّ فَاحْذَرْهُمْ ؕ قٰتَلَهُمُ اللّٰهُ ۫ أَنّٰى يُؤْفَكُوْنَ

When they are told, 'Come forward and Allāh's Messenger will seek forgiveness for you,' they turn their heads around and you see them arrogantly turning away.	5	وَإِذَا قِيلَ لَهُمْ تَعَالَوْا يَسْتَغْفِرْ لَكُمْ رَسُولُ اللّٰهِ لَوَّوْا رُءُوسَهُمْ وَرَأَيْتَهُمْ يَصُدُّونَ وَهُمْ مُّسْتَكْبِرُونَ
It is the same to them whether you seek forgiveness for them or whether you do not seek forgiveness for them. Allāh shall never forgive them. Verily Allāh does not guide the sinful ones."	6	سَوَآءٌ عَلَيْهِمْ أَسْتَغْفَرْتَ لَهُمْ أَمْ لَمْ تَسْتَغْفِرْ لَهُمْ ؕ لَنْ يَّغْفِرَ اللّٰهُ لَهُمْ ؕ إِنَّ اللّٰهَ لَا يَهْدِي الْقَوْمَ الْفٰسِقِيْنَ
They are the ones who said, 'Do not spend on those with the Messenger of Allāh until they disperse.' To Allāh belongs the treasures of the heavens and the earth but the hypocrites do not under-	7	هُمُ الَّذِيْنَ يَقُوْلُوْنَ لَا تُنْفِقُوْا عَلٰى مَنْ عِنْدَ رَسُوْلِ اللّٰهِ حَتّٰى يَنْفَضُّوْا ؕ وَلِلّٰهِ خَزَآئِنُ السَّمٰوٰتِ وَالْأَرْضِ وَلٰكِنَّ الْمُنٰفِقِيْنَ لَا يَفْقَهُوْنَ
They say, 'If we return to Madīnah , the honourable ones among us shall certainly exile the humiliated ones. All honour belongs to Allāh, His Messenger and the believers but the Munāfiqūn do not know it.	8	يَقُوْلُوْنَ لَئِنْ رَّجَعْنَآ إِلَى الْمَدِيْنَةِ لَيُخْرِجَنَّ الْأَعَزُّ مِنْهَا الْأَذَلَّ ؕ وَلِلّٰهِ الْعِزَّةُ وَلِرَسُوْلِهٖ وَلِلْمُؤْمِنِيْنَ وَلٰكِنَّ الْمُنٰفِقِيْنَ لَا يَعْلَمُوْنَ

O you who have īmān! Let not your wealth and your children make you neglect Allāh's remembrance. Those who do this are certainly losers.	9	يٰٓاَيُّهَا الَّذِيْنَ اٰمَنُوْا لَا تُلْهِكُمْ اَمْوَالُكُمْ وَلَآ اَوْلَادُكُمْ عَنْ ذِكْرِ اللّٰهِ ۚ وَمَنْ يَّفْعَلْ ذٰلِكَ فَاُولٰٓئِكَ هُمُ الْخٰسِرُوْنَ
Spend from what We have provided for you before death comes to any of you and then he says, 'O my Lord! Why do you not grant me respite for a little while longer so that I can spend in charity and become of the righteous.'	10	وَاَنْفِقُوْا مِنْ مَّا رَزَقْنٰكُمْ مِّنْ قَبْلِ اَنْ يَّاْتِيَ اَحَدَكُمُ الْمَوْتُ فَيَقُوْلَ رَبِّ لَوْلَآ اَخَّرْتَنِيْٓ اِلٰٓى اَجَلٍ قَرِيْبٍ ۙ فَاَصَّدَّقَ وَاَكُنْ مِّنَ الصّٰلِحِيْنَ
Allāh shall not grant respite to any soul when its term arrives. Allāh is Informed of what you do.	11	وَلَنْ يُّؤَخِّرَ اللّٰهُ نَفْسًا اِذَا جَآءَ اَجَلُهَا ۭ وَاللّٰهُ خَبِيْرٌۢ بِمَا تَعْمَلُوْنَ

بحمد الله تم

Quranic Wonders

The science of Tafsīr in itself is very vast, hence the compilation of these specific verses provides the reader with a simple and brief commentary. It is aimed to equip the reader with a small glimpse of the profound beauty of the Holy Qur'ān so that they can gain the passion to study further in depth. It is hoped that this will become a means of encouragement to increase the zeal and enthusiasm to recite and inculcate the teachings of the Holy Qur'ān into our daily lives. **UK RRP:£5:00**

Protection in the Grave

Sūrah Al-Mulk encapsulates the purpose of our creation - that we were created to live a life of obedience to our Lord and Creator. This can only be made to manifest through our good deeds which we perform solely for the sake of Allāh ﷻ, in order to seek His pleasure. The Holy Prophet ﷺ told his Ummah to recite this Sūrah every night and learn this Sūrah by heart. The importance of this Sūrah is stressed due to the fact that the Holy Prophet ﷺ never slept until he had finished reciting this Sūrah. **UK RRP:£4:00**

Protection from Black Magic

These last ten Sūrahs are not only distinct in their meanings and message which will be discussed in this book, but also the fact that every Muslim should have these Sūrahs committed to memory as a minimum requirement in seeking refuge in Allāh ﷻ from all harm and evil, and every imperfection as well as seeking solace and peace in understanding His might and attributes. **UK RRP:£5:00**

ırturing Children in Islam

'inging up children has never been an easy duty. The challenges do not t easier as they get older either. Our emotions and other priorities metimes hinder in nurturing our children, and as such, we fail to as- ;t our children in reaching their potential by continually stumbling 'er our own perception of what we consider as ideal children. Our duty our children is not without accountability. Our neglect and lack of terest in our children will be held to task. **UK RRP:£5:00**

Best of Stories
Sūrah Yūsuf is more than just a story of one of our beloved Prophets there is much wisdom and lessons to be learnt and understood. All t knowledge comes from our honourable Shaykh, inspiration and Ustā Shaykh Mufti Saiful Islām Sāhib. May Allāh shower Mufti Sāhib wi mercy and accept the day in, day out effort he carries out in the work Dīn. **UK RRP:£4:00**

Call of Nuh
For 950 years, Sayyidunā Nūh persevered night and day in continuous succession in preaching the message; unwavering and relentless in his mission. Not once did he feel that his calling was in vain. He stood firm and resolute in continuing with the mission that he was sent with, in proclaiming the message of the oneness of Allāh ; year after year, decade upon decade, century after century, but this failed to convince the people of the truth. **UK RRP:£4:00**

A Glimpse of Paradise
Time is the true wealth we have at our disposal though it cannot be amassed. The only way we can utilise it to our advantage is when we do righteous deeds and actions; for this will act in our favour in the Ākhirah (Hereafter). These moments will be preserved in exchange for moments of greater happiness and bliss in the next life. Therefore, we need to perform righteous deeds and actions in the short duration of time we have at our disposal in this temporary worldly life.

UK RRP:£4:00

Six Qualities of a Believer
Respected readers, do you want to be successful in this life and the Hereafter? The fact that you have prompted yourself to pick up this book and read, is an indication that the answer is *yes*. Or perhaps, you were not aware of the contents and purpose of this book and hence, eternal success wasn't the first thing on your mind. Nonetheless, it is easy to turn your attention towards this objective right now. **UK RRP:£2:00**

Ready for Judgement Day?
For those that doubt the Day of Resurrection, Allāh ﷻ is reaffirming that there is no scope for uncertainty; this day is indisputable and will surely occur. The day when the truth will be laid out bare and everything will be exposed, there will be no place to flee or escape to. Regretting that day will be of no avail; excuses will fail to safeguard or shelter a person from breaking free and escaping judgement. **UK RRP:£4:00**

Flee Towards Allāh ﷻ
Sūrah Al-Ma'ārij begins by addressing the disbelievers who used to mock the Holy Prophet ﷺ about the Day of Judgement. In this Surah, Allāh ﷻ severely reproaches those who deny it assuming that there is only one life; the life of this world. The Sūrah manifests its horrors and catastrophic scenes that the entire creation shall witness on that very day. Mankind will then realise that on this horrific day, they will be judged by their own actions. **UK RRP:£4:00**

Lanterns of Knowledge
Once the commentary of Kitābul 'Ilm in Bukhāri was completed, we realised that this chapter is an entire topic in itself due to its fascinating and insightful perspective on knowledge. When compiling this commentary, there were many beautiful reminders as well as points of guidance for everyone's personal life as well as their lifelong quest for knowledge. Therefore, the commentary of this chapter alone would be beneficial for all seekers of knowledge and the idea of publishing it as a separate book came to mind. **UK RRP:£10:00**

TIME IS RUNNING OUT
As the title suggests, as each day passes, we come closer to our death. Life is too short to be treated as an amusement and for the fulfillment of one's lust. The Day of Judgement is inevitable where we all must one day stand in front of the Lord of the Worlds to give an account of our deeds. These six Sūrahs explain the horrors and terrifying moments of Judgement Day and the inevitable standing before the Lord. We must therefore prepare for the Hereafter by realizing our purpose in life; to worship Allāh ﷻ Alone and reduce our worldly expectations. **UK RRP:£4:00**

Living Islām in Modern Times

This book is a compilation of various articles written by Shaykh D Rafāqat Rashīd Sāhib in the popular Al-Mu'min Magazine. Conside ing the great benefit these articles will bring to the Ummah, Mu Saiful Islām Sāhib decided to edit and transform them into a bo format, making the content easily accessible for readers.

UK RRP:£4:0

A CLEAR VICTORY

This book "A Clear Victory" is an enlightening commentary of Sūrah Al-Fath. It is cited in Sahīh Al-Bukhāri regarding the virtue of this Sūrah that Sayyidunā Umar Ibn Al-Khattāb ﷺ reported that the Messenger of Allāh ﷺ said: "This night a Sūrah was sent down to me that is more beloved to me than all what the sun shines over," then he read, "*We have indeed accorded a triumph to you, a manifest triumph, indeed*". **UK RRP:£5:00**